# AWAY from the MANGER

## 15 Sketches for Christmases in the 21st Century

## Les Ellison

NIMBUS
Press

Published by Nimbus Press,
18 Guilford Road, Leicester, LE2 2RB.
Tel. 0116 270 6318
Web site: http://www.nimbuspress.co.uk
Email: publisher@nimbuspress.co.uk


*Cover illustration by Polly Deal.*

British Library Cataloguing in Publication
Data available


ISBN 1 874424 77 2


Printed in Great Britain by
Cambrian Printers, Llanbadarn Road, Aberystwyth, SY23 3TN

# AWAY from the MANGER

## 15 Sketches for Christmases in the 21st Century

### Les Ellison

The story of the baby in the manger has been presented for so long as something for the children, that grown-ups have forgotten that the truth of the story is for them. In two thousand years of telling and retelling the grown-up world has moved so far from the manger that the story is now as much a part of childhood fiction as Santa Claus and flying reindeer. But what about the truth? Is it time for Christians to stop defending the childhood fiction and remind the world of the grown-up truth?

# Performance and Copyright

# CONTENTS

# INTRODUCTION

As publishers we receive a constant stream of manuscripts based on the birth stories in Matthew and Luke. Some of these stories (particularly in Matthew) were written to persuade Jewish people that Jesus really was the Messiah, although he was very different from the warrior-king whom they expected. Other stories showed that he came for marginalised people (the shepherds) and foreigners (the wise men.)

These stories have become part of our folklore and children still have fun dressing up (or grandparents enjoy seeing their little Emily pretending to be a sheep.) The truths that they tell are still important, though most Christians today do not have any difficulty in believing that Jesus was sent by God and that he came for all people.

But they are stories. Only those who start out with an unshakeable belief that the whole Bible is literally true could mistake them for history. They cannot both be historically accurate because they contradict each other. Matthew, for example, tells us that Joseph and Mary lived in Bethlehem and that Jesus was born in his parents' home there. Luke says that they had to travel from their home in Nazareth and that Jesus was born in a stable.

In these sketches Les Ellison tries to explore the mysteries of what God has done for us all through Jesus, in stories that are related to our world in the twenty-first century.

If you would like some further material on this theme, perhaps for a talk or service illustrated by the sketches, then two useful resources that inspired Les Ellison are *Meeting Jesus AGAIN for the First Time* (SPCK) by Marcus J Borg and 'Not in Front of the Children'(Nimbus Press - available direct from the publisher) by Clifford Sharp.

Clifford Sharp, July 2002

......................

Partly based on thoughts and ideas in
*Meeting Jesus AGAIN for the First Time* (SPCK)
by **Marcus J Borg**
Professor of Religion and Culture at Oregon State University.
and on
**'Not in Front of the Children'**
(Nimbus Press 'Square One' imprint)
by **Clifford Sharp**

......................

# 1. ALL QUIET ON THE CHRISTMAS FRONT

Characters
### The Colonel
*A senior officer of the 'old school'.*
### Carstairs
*An officer; the colonel's Aide de Camp.*
### Ginny
*An officer in the Women's Royal Army Corps.*

*The setting appears to be a trench on the western front, in the winter of 1914. The style is that of a British 'stiff upper lip' film intended to boost the morale of a nation with its back to the wall. Token military headwear, such as caps, steel helmets or balaclavas, and blankets will cover for any absence of authentic uniforms.*

**The Colonel** *is alone, nursing an injured arm in a makeshift sling.* **Carstairs** *enters.*

**Colonel**    Who goes there?

**Carstairs**    It's me, Sir.

**Colonel**    Carstairs. Thank God. Thought you were one of theirs, back to finish us off.

**Carstairs**    No, Sir. Just me, Sir. Managed to scrounge a biscuit. And I've made some tea in this Bully Beef tin. *(Offers this to the* **Colonel***.)*

**Colonel**    Good man. Good man. *(Accepting and drinking the tea.)*

**Carstairs**    Do you ... do you know what day it is, Sir?

| Colonel | Can't say I do, Carstairs. Each day seems very much like another in this hell. |

| Carstairs | It's December the twenty-fourth, Sir. Christmas Eve. |

| Colonel | Christmas Eve ... they said it would all be over by Christmas. |

| Carstairs | Sir. |

| Colonel | God, what a mess. How many left? |

| Carstairs | Serving, Sir? You. Me ... And Ginny. Sir. |

| Colonel | Ginny. Damn. This is no place for a woman. And the others? |

| Carstairs | Gone Sir. All ... gone. |

*Ginny enters. She has the cheery spirit of resilience despite the hard times.*

| Ginny | Hello Sir. *(Saluting the **Colonel**.)* |

| Carstairs | I say, it's Ginny, Sir. |

| Colonel | Hello, Ginny. |

| Ginny | Hello, Carstairs. What's the picture? |

| Carstairs | Pretty grim, I'm afraid. |

| Colonel | Grim? It's a ruddy shambles, that's what it is. Christmas Eve. Only two officers left to man the tills. And out there, ten thousand last minute shoppers; stocking up |

and ready to storm the checkouts and break right through to the car park

**Ginny**    Three officers, Sir. I can handle a cash register.

**Carstairs**    Ginny, you can't. You're too ... delicatessen.

**Ginny**    I'm not afraid, Sir. I've done my bit on the meat counter.

**Colonel**    That's the spirit. God, I wish I had more men like you. *(He gestures with his injured arm and winces at the pain.)*

**Ginny**    Arm giving you gyp, sir?

**Colonel**    Touch of the old 'RSI', that's all. Damn frozen turkeys. Those twenty-four pounders take some handling.

**Carstairs**    Yes, Sir. They knock the stuffing into them.

**Ginny**    Take a look at it, if you like, Sir. *(She tends to his arm.)*

*The sound of voices singing the carol 'Silent Night, Holy Night' in German.*

**Carstairs**    Listen, Sir. They're ... singing.

**Colonel**    Good God. So they are.

**Ginny**    Silent Night, Holy Night. All is calm. All is bright.

**Colonel**    You could almost believe they were just like us.

**Carstairs**    Perhaps you could ... read us something, Sir. From ... The Book. We know you keep one.

| | |
|---|---|
| **Colonel** | The Book? Yes. Yes, I do. Call me an old fool but ... *(Produces a Bible from an inside pocket.)* I don't know, when the chips are down ... |
| **Carstairs** | Chips do that to a man, Sir. |
| **Ginny** | Go on, Sir. We'd appreciate it. |
| **Colonel** | *(Takes off his hat, opens his Bible and reads.)* Something from the Profit ... 'And he shall judge among the nations and shall rebuke many people. And they shall beat their baskets into plough-shares, and their trolleys into pruning hooks. Nation shall not lift up credit against nation, neither shall they learn consumerism anymore.' |
| **Carstairs** | Amen. |
| **Ginny** | Do you think ... Do you think it will ever happen, Sir? |
| **Colonel** | I don't know, Ginny. One day, perhaps. One day. If we try hard, and stand our ground. |
| **Carstairs** | *(Breaking down.)* What gets me, Sir ... What gets me is the ruddy waste of it all. |
| **Colonel** | Steady, Carstairs ... |
| **Carstairs** | It's all so damned unnecessary! |

*The singing fades and stops.*

| | |
|---|---|
| **Ginny** | It's alright, Sir. *(Comforting **Carstairs**.)* He's been too long in the aisles. He's just a bit ... shelf shocked. |
| **Carstairs** | Listen. |

**Colonel**    It's quiet. Too quiet.

**Ginny**    They've stopped singing.

**Colonel**    Well, this looks like it then. Better check your magazines.

*They each produce a publication from within their blankets.*

**Carstairs**    Radio Times.

**Ginny**    Woman's Weekly.

**Colonel**    FHM. Good. Till Rolls?

**Carstairs**    Four, Sir. Maybe five.

**Ginny**    Three, Sir.

**Colonel**    Very good. And Ginny, don't forget; save the last one for yourself.

**Ginny**    Sir.

**Colonel**    Carstairs, take the ten-items-or-less. Ginny, the wheelchair access. I'll take enquiries and returns. Good luck everyone.

**Carstairs**    Good luck, Sir.

**Ginny**    Good luck.

**Colonel**    Oh, and erm ... Merry Christmas everyone.

**Carstairs & Ginny** *(Together.)* Merry Christmas, Sir.

*Colonel stands, checks his watch and places a whistle between his lips. Carstairs and Ginny remove their blankets or greatcoats to reveal supermarket checkout overalls.*

**Colonel**    Right. On your feet. Fix nametags!

*The three of them pin their name badges to their overalls. Colonel checks his watch then blows the whistle and the three of them charge off holding their rolled up magazines as guns. Colonel is left standing alone. He takes out his Bible and taps it on the palm of his hand.*

**Colonel**    Wonder what He'd say; if he saw us going over the top every Christmas.


END

# 2. HEIRS AND GRACES

## Characters
**Sir John**
*A conscientious Lord of the manor.*
**Jennings**
*A disgruntled employee on Sir John's estate.*

*Sir John is preoccupied with several official looking letters and statements of account. He has a gift-wrapped pair of slippers under one arm. Jennings enters.*

**Jennings**    I've put the car away, Sir. Thought it best to change the tyres. Top of the estate always gets bad around the year's end. Don't want to get snowed in for Christmas do we? Not with the boy coming home.

**Sir John**    *(Without looking up.)* No. No. Good idea. Thank you.

**Jennings**    Expect you'll be pleased to have him home. Doing well, is he?

**Sir John**    Yes. Yes, thank you. *(Still engrossed in his papers.)* We have err ... great hopes for him ... yes ...

**Jennings**    Will that be all, Sir John?

**Sir John**    What? Oh, yes. Yes, that'll be all, Jennings.

**Jennings**    I'll be off then now, shall I?

*Sir John looks up at Jennings, who draws Sir John's attention to the gift-wrapped parcel.*

| | |
|---|---|
| **Sir John** | Sorry, sorry. Completely forgot. *(Offers the parcel to Jennings.)* Merry Christmas, Jennings. |
| **Jennings** | Oh, thank you, Sir. Shall I open it now or wait 'til tomorrow? |
| **Sir John** | You can open it now if you like. |

*Jennings opens the parcel.*

| | |
|---|---|
| **Jennings** | Slippers. Thank you. Very kind. Very kind indeed. Choose them yourself did you, Sir? Or did you send someone out for them? |
| **Sir John** | I'm sorry? |
| **Jennings** | Slippers. Doesn't show that much imagination does it, Sir? Not much thought, if you know what I mean. Not much of a show of gratitude. |
| **Sir John** | It's not meant to be a show ... |
| **Jennings** | ... Obviously. |
| **Sir John** | It's Christmas. |
| **Jennings** | Yes, it's Christmas. And at Christmas, people like you like to remind people like me who people like me really are. Don't you? |
| **Sir John** | Come on, Jennings, you know that's hardly fair. |
| **Jennings** | No, it's not fair. It's not a bit fair. Look at you; with your bank accounts and your investments and your business plans ... |

| | |
|---|---|
| **Sir John** | And my bills and my debts and my mortgage. The estate doesn't run itself, you know. |
| **Jennings** | I know. I'm out there running it. While you're up here in your big house, I'm out there building walls, mending fences and fixing gates. Well you can keep your slippers. |
| **Sir John** | Pardon? |
| **Jennings** | I said, keep your slippers. Keep 'em. I don't want 'em. I don't need slippers. Do you think I need your slippers? 'Cos I don't. I got everything I need. Me and my missus. |
| **Sir John** | Yes, I know. |
| **Jennings** | How do you know? You don't know me. You don't know my life. How do you know what I need? |
| **Sir John** | Well, because I pay you. And your wife. I provide your cottage, your gas and electric, eggs, milk, butter, the use of the landrover. And a pension. |
| **Jennings** | Yeah. Well. Still don't need your slippers. |
| **Sir John** | Look, forget the slippers. I'm sorry, I'll take them back. I just wanted to give you something. For Christmas. |
| **Jennings** | Alright. |
| **Sir John** | Alright what? |
| **Jennings** | Give me something. |
| **Sir John** | What would you like? |
| **Jennings** | The boy. |

**Sir John**    What?

**Jennings**    I said the boy. Your son. Give me your son.

**Sir John**    Don't be ridiculous.

**Jennings**    I work for you, he can work for me.

**Sir John**    You can't afford a servant.

**Jennings**    Then you'll need to pay me better, won't you?

**Sir John**    Alright. I'll raise your salary. (*Moves to give him some money from his wallet. Then ...*) No. If you're taking him you can take it all. All of it. There.

*Sir John gives Jennings all the money, the wallet, and the papers.*

**Jennings**    What?

**Sir John**    It would have passed to him one day. If you're his Master then I suppose it's yours now.

**Jennings**    All of it?

**Sir John**    Yes.

**Jennings**    House, title, estate?

**Sir John**    Everything. Well everything I can give you.

**Jennings**    Meaning?

**Sir John**    There is a ... wisdom to looking after it all properly.

**Jennings**    Then tell it me.

**Sir John**   I've been trying for years. You won't listen to me.

**Jennings**   You can't just leave me; not with all this. *(The papers.)*

**Sir John**   You have the boy. Just watch what he does and do the same, though I doubt if it's your idea of wisdom.

**Jennings**   What are you talking about?

**Sir John**   Well, the first thing he'll do is take down all your walls and fences, and open up the gates.

**Jennings**   What?

**Sir John**   Yes. Should have settled for the slippers shouldn't you? *(Makes to leave. Then turns back to **Jennings**.)* Oh, and erm ... Merry Christmas.

***Sir John** leaves. **Jennings** stands alone.*

## END

# 3. LIBERTY BODICE

## Characters
### *Pam*
*A fashion conscious Christmas reveller.*
### *Trish*
*Her best friend.*

**Trish**   So, you going to the Christmas party then, or what?

**Pam**   Might.

**Trish**   Oh, go on. You'll love it.

**Pam**   Mmm ... alright then.

**Trish**   T'riffic. What you going to wear then?

**Pam**   Might wear my new jacket.

**Trish**   What, is it sort of all sparkly and really tight fitting?

**Pam**   Well, it's really tight fitting.

**Trish**   You mean sort of stretchy vinyl sort of thing?

**Pam**   No, sort of heavy duty canvas sort of thing ...

**Trish**   Canvas?

**Pam**   With sort of really big buckles and leather straps.

**Trish**   What kind of jacket's that?

**Pam**   It's a straitjacket.

| | |
|---|---|
| **Trish** | What, like they used to have in lunatic asylums? |
| **Pam** | Yeah. It's really strong. The sleeves buckle to your waist so you can't move your arms. |
| **Trish** | Isn't that a bit ... restrictive? |
| **Pam** | Oh, yes. That's the whole idea, isn't it? |
| **Trish** | Is it? How do you do anything in it, how do you feed yourself? |
| **Pam** | You don't. You just eat whatever gets put in your mouth. And you can't drive, least not safely. So you have to go wherever you're taken, whether you want to or not. |
| **Trish** | Don't fancy that. |
| **Pam** | No, it's t'riffic, it is. You don't have to do anything for yourself. You don't have to decide anything, you don't even have to think for yourself. |
| **Trish** | Ooh, you're right, I never thought of that. Here, I'm going to get myself one of them. |
| **Pam** | And wear it to the party? |
| **Trish** | No, I'm going to save it 'til Christmas Day. At last: something I can wear that won't be out of place in church. Even at Christmas. |

END

# 4. EXODUS TRAVEL

## Characters

**Agent**
*Travel agent*
**Trav 1**
*A traveller, looking to book a guided tour.*
**Trav 2**
*Traveller 1's companion.*

*Trav 1 and 2 are waiting for the Agent to return to his desk or office.*

**Agent**    *(Enters.)* Well, I think I've found one.

**Trav 1**    At last.

**Agent**    It wasn't easy.

**Trav 2**    But you did find one?

**Agent**    There's not a lot of call ...

**Trav 1**    Yes, we know.

**Trav 2**    Though you'd have thought everyone would ...

**Agent**    Oh, yes. Everyone wants to *be* there, but not many actually want to *go*; make the journey, that is.

**Trav 1**    That's why we wanted a guide ...

**Agent**    Very wise. It's a bit of a wilderness out there, by all accounts.

| | |
|---|---|
| **Trav 2** | Yes, someone who knows the way. |
| **Trav 1** | And can take us straight there. |
| **Agent** | Yes. Well, as I said, it's a bit ... difficult. |
| **Trav 2** | Difficult? |
| **Agent** | Yes. |
| **Trav 1** | But you did say you'd found someone? |
| **Agent** | Oh, yes. I found ... someone. |
| **Trav 2** | Who's been there before? |
| **Agent** | Well ... no ... |
| **Trav 1** | But he knows where it is? |
| **Agent** | Not exactly ... But he does know what it looks like. Or what it should look like. |
| **Trav 2** | I think we'd better meet him. |
| **Agent** | Well that's a bit difficult too. |
| **Trav 1** | But I thought you just ... |
| **Agent** | Ah. No. No, he's not ... here. |
| **Trav 2** | Then ... where? |
| **Agent** | Out … there. |
| **Trav 1** | You mean he started without us? |

| | |
|---|---|
| **Agent** | He wants to get there too, you know. |
| **Trav 2** | So what are we supposed to do; hang around waiting for him to come back? |
| **Agent** | Oh no. Don't wait for him to come back. When he comes back it'll be too late. I think you should start right away. |
| **Trav 1** | Perhaps we should think about it. Maybe leave it 'til next year. |
| **Agent** | Well that's up to you, but the longer you leave it, the more difficult it is just to get started, believe me. |
| **Trav 2** | How will we know if we're on the right path? |
| **Agent** | Bit of advice; don't look for *the path*. Look for *the guide*. Look for him. When you find him, you'll know you're on the right track. Couldn't be easier. |

*Agent begins to usher the **travellers** gently out of his office.*

Oh, and err ... don't worry. *(Without sarcasm)* Just enjoy the trip. It's quite an adventure, believe me. *(Watches them leave.)*

## END

# 5. CHRISTMAS WISHES

### Characters
**Dreamer**
*Learning his part for a carol service.*
**Schemer**
*Writing his list for Father Christmas.*

*__Schemer__ is sitting puzzling over, and writing, his Christmas wish list. __Dreamer__ is reading and trying to memorise a passage from the Bible.*

**Dreamer**   'Unto us a boy is born.'

**Schemer**   A bike. Off-road. Adjustable front and rear shocks. Silver.

**Dreamer**   'And his name shall be called Wonderful, Counsellor.'

**Schemer**   Playstation 2 with ... *(Whatever the most wanted games happen to be.)*

**Dreamer**   'The mighty God!'

**Schemer**   Walkman MP3 Minidisk player-recorder, and ...

**Dreamer**   'The Everlasting Father' ... what else ...? *(Consulting his script.)*

**Schemer**   Oh, yeah. Scalextric. Formula One, with lap counter and double chicane.

**Dreamer**   'The Prince of Peace.'

**Schemer**   And a drum kit. Twelve piece. Anything loud.

**Dreamer**   'Of the increase of his government and ... peace ... there shall be no end.'

**Schemer**   *(Finished writing.)* That is truly inspired.

**Dreamer**   It's coming. I'll have it by the carol service.

**Schemer**   Not you. This. My Christmas list. *(Hands it over.)*

**Dreamer**   *(Reading.)* 'Dear Father Christmas ...' Aren't you a bit old for this?

**Schemer**   You're never too old to believe.

**Dreamer**   Or too stupid, apparently.

**Schemer**   I'm too old for that rubbish you've been spouting.

**Dreamer**   It's not rubbish. It's a prophecy.

**Schemer**   When does it happen then?

**Dreamer**   Christmas.

**Schemer**   Any Christmas in particular?

**Dreamer**   The first Christmas, stupid.

**Schemer**   'Peace without end.' Well I'm glad you told me, 'cos I'd never have noticed. You know, what with the Middle East, and *(other current wars or conflicts.)*

**Dreamer**   Alright. It's an ideal, but it's going to happen.

**Schemer**     And you're waiting for it to fall down the chimney into your stocking?

**Dreamer**     It's in the Bible. It's not a made up wish list to a made up fat guy in a red suit.

**Schemer**     Yeah, but if I show this to the right people, say the right things, do a few favours, I might end up with one out of five, maybe two, and that's in just one Christmas. Look at your list. How many wishes have you made come true? None. And in how many Christmases? Two thousand?

**Dreamer**     It's a vision.

**Schemer**     It's a dream. What you've got is a dream. But what you haven't got is any idea how to make it all come true.

END

# 6. GOD BLESS US, EVERY ONE.

### Characters
**Host**
*The host of a genteel, suburban Christmas dinner.*
**Wife**
*The host's wife.*
**Guests**
*Two guests at the dinner, perhaps a couple.*

*The **Host**, his **Wife**, and their **Two Guests** have just finished their Christmas dinner. They are still wearing their Christmas-cracker party hats as they relax with coffees and/ or a glass of wine.*

**Host**      ... Of course, what I really like about Christmas is, it's universal. I mean, it's for everyone, isn't it? Yes? It doesn't matter who you are, everybody celebrates Christmas.

**Wife**      Except Jews.

**Host**      What?

**Wife**      Jews don't celebrate Christmas.

**Guest 1**   No. Nor Muslims.

**Guest 2**   Or Sikhs, and Buddhists ...

**Host**      ... I mean Christians; everybody who's a Christian, obviously. If you're a Christian, then it doesn't matter who you are. On the twenty-fifth of December, you celebrate Christmas.

| | |
|---|---|
| **Wife** | Unless you're Orthodox. |
| **Guest 1** | Or Coptic. |
| **Guest 2** | Or Albanian. |
| **Wife** | In which case, you're on the Julian calendar, and celebrate Christmas on the sixth of January. |
| **Host** | What I'm trying to say is, if you're a Christian, and not Orthodox ... |
| **Guest 2** | ... or Albanian. |
| **Host** | Or Albanian, then you celebrate the twenty-fifth of December as the birth of Jesus Christ the Son of God. |
| **Wife** | Not if you're a Unitarian. |
| **Guest 1** | Or a follower of Servetus and Sozzini ... |
| **Guest 2** | ... who denied the divinity of Christ and the doctrine of the Trinity ... |
| **Host** | Well obviously, not if you deny the Trinity, but if you're a Christian, and none of those ... other things, you can sit down together, in your own home ... |
| **Wife** | ... if you've got one. |
| **Host** | ... and enjoy a roast turkey ... |
| **Guest 1** | ... not if you're a vegetarian. |
| **Host** | ... a bottle of wine. |

**Guest 2**    Unless you're an alcoholic.

**Host**    … and all the trimmings.

**Wife**    If you can afford them these days.

**Host**    Yes. Yes, alright! Alright. *(Struggling to keep control of himself.)* What I mean is … If you're a middle class, home owning, meat eating, mainstream Christian – in the western tradition – with no theological disputes or antisocial tendencies, then Christmas, right, meaning Jesus Christ … is just for you.

**Guest 1**    Why's that then? Why especially for us?

**Host**    Well, it's because we appreciate him most, obviously

**Wife**    No, it's because we need him most. Obviously.


### END

# 7. MADONNA

## Characters
### *Mary*
*The mother of Jesus.*

*Mary* stands alone, her back to the audience, cradling a 'baby' in her arms. She wears the traditional 'Mary' costume pulled up over a modern hair style and fashionable t-shirt top which she reveals as she turns to the audience before her speech begins. She has the attitude of a modern, independent girl in her late teens/early twenties and addresses the audience with the credibility, confidence and determination of a street-wise young woman.

**Mary**      Well? What did you expect? A halo? A nimbus? A golden glow? Then I'm sorry to disappoint you. I never had one. They gave me that; Giotto, Da Vinci, Botticelli. And the rest. It's amazing what people expect of you these days. A halo. A title. 'Saint', 'Holy Mother'. 'Holy Virgin'. Yes. Because that's what this is about isn't it?

Go on then. Ask me. It's what you want to know isn't it? Was I a virgin? Don't look away. Was I a virgin? I know. I can see it. I've been seeing it for two thousand years. I know all the arguments, I've heard all the debates. And sometimes, I think it's all that matters to you, isn't it?

Never mind what it was like to live with him; my son. To bring him up. To hear the things he said. Things that never got written down because there was no one there to hear them. Except me. Things that you'll never know.

Never mind all that. Never mind what it was like to watch him die. No. Never mind any of that. What you want to know is; was I a virgin?

Well, what if I was? What if I wasn't? What's it to you? Does it matter so much to you? Because it didn't matter to him. I mattered to him, that's all, and if you need me to measure up to your ideal, your image of what it means to be acceptable to God, then that's your problem, not mine.

And not his.

*Mary* tends affectionately to the 'baby' and turns away from the audience.

## END

# 8. THE GOSPEL ACCORDING TO SAINT FUDGE

## Characters

**Editor**
*Tasked with compiling the Christmas story*
**Matthew**
*The gospel writer – of the version with the wise men*
**Luke**
*The gospel writer – of the version with the shepherds*
**Marketing**
*A smart and perceptive woman from that department*

*Matthew and Luke are talking quietly together. They have been in a long meeting. Editor enters with a sheaf of papers and accompanied by Marketing.*

**Editor**  OK. Let's have one more try, shall we? And this time, let's see if we can't exercise a little give and take. You know "compromise"?

**Matthew**  Hold it a second. Who's she?

**Editor**  I borrowed her from marketing.

**Luke**  You said this was a sure-fire best-seller. How come we need marketing?

**Editor**  We just need a fresh brain on this. Someone who hasn't listened to you two arguing for the last … too long.

*Matthew and Luke exchange glances, then shrug or nod their reluctant consent.*

| | |
|---|---|
| **Editor** | OK. For the sake of those who are new to this, *(acknowledges **Marketing**)* let's go over it one more time from the beginning: Matthew; you got Jesus being born in his parents house in Bethlehem, and Luke; you got his parents living in Nazareth and travelling to Bethlehem? |
| **Luke** | Yes. |
| **Editor** | Good. So Jesus was born in Bethlehem. At least we got that agreed. |
| **Mkting** | Unless it was Nazareth. |
| **Editor** | What? |
| **Mkting** | Well. If he was born in his parents' house, which is what Matthew says, but they lived in Nazareth, which is what Luke says, then he was born in Nazareth. |
| **Editor** | I thought I asked you here to find agreement. |
| **Mkting** | Sorry, I was just trying to establish the facts. |
| **Editor** | You're in marketing; what do you now about facts? OK. What else have we got? |
| **Luke** | The census. |
| **Matthew** | What census? |
| **Luke** | The census that made it necessary for Mary and Joseph to travel from Nazareth to Bethlehem. |

| | |
|---|---|
| **Mkting** | While Mary was pregnant ... |
| **Matthew** | There was no census in 4BC, when Herod was King in Judea. |
| **Luke** | But there was in 6AD, when Quirinius was Governor in Syria. |
| **Matthew** | Herod was dead in 6AD. |
| **Mkting** | And Mary was pregnant for ten years ... *(In response to a withering look from **Editor**)…* apparently. |
| **Editor** | OK. So we can't agree on where he was born, or when exactly, but we do know that, wherever it was, it was a stable ... |
| **Matthew** | I never said that. Luke said a stable, not me. |
| **Luke** | I never said stable. I said manger. I said 'they laid him in a manger.' I never said the manger was in a stable. |
| **Editor** | Jeez! OK. What about ... *(Reading his copy.)* the star… |
| **Luke** | ... That's Matthew's star. I never said there was a star. |
| **Editor** | ... that guides the three kings? |
| **Matthew** | I said wise men; magi. And I never said how many. |
| **Luke** | Sloppy, I call that. Sloppy writing. |
| **Matthew** | You never said how many shepherds. |
| **Luke** | It doesn't matter how many shepherds. |

| | |
|---|---|
| **Editor** | Hey. Get focused here. They're banging on my door. They're shouting for the true story. I got to give them something. I got to give them Luke or Matthew. |
| **Mkting** | Why not give them Luke *and* Matthew? |
| **Editor** | You mean fudge it? |
| **Mkting** | Luke's manger, the census, Mary on a donkey, Matthew's star and the travellers from the East. Add the stable, a few animals. Call it 'The Nativity.' |
| **Editor** | This is no two-bit story we're doing here, this is the big one. This is about God and his creation. And you two can't even agree on what actually happened! |
| **Matthew** | Actually happened? |
| **Editor** | *(Giving up.)* Jeez ... |
| **Luke** | You want ... what actually happened? |
| **Editor** | 'Course I want what actually happened. |

*Luke* and *Matthew* exchange glances.

| | |
|---|---|
| **Matthew** | We thought you wanted the truth, not ... what actually happened. |

## END

# 9. UNRECORDED DELIVERY

## Characters

**Junior**
*A young midwife, just starting her career.*
**Senior**
*An older midwife, just finishing her career.*

*The **two midwives** stand together. They might each wear a simple white headscarf and plain dress to denote their vocation. They have just finished delivering the baby that the **junior midwife** holds with keen affection.*

**Junior**    You're sure about this?

**Senior**    Yes. I think it's about time.

**Junior**    There's nothing I can say to change your mind?

**Senior**    No. But thank you.

**Junior**    How do you decide; when to retire I mean? Do you say… one thousand? Two thousand?

**Senior**    You just get tired, that's all.

**Junior**    You're a midwife – and a good one.

**Senior**    Even good midwives get tired. Eventually.

**Junior**    Well I don't know how can you tire of delivering babies? I'll never get tired.

**Senior**    That's what I said. When I was your age.

| | |
|---|---|
| **Junior** | You delivered me, didn't you? You'd have been about my age then ... I suppose. |
| **Senior** | I might have done. Probably. I can't remember. |
| **Junior** | Can't remember? |
| **Senior** | I can't remember them all. Can't remember half of them. Half of a half of them. The difficult ones, I remember those. And the ones that were ... well, a little too difficult. |
| **Junior** | Do you remember your first? |
| **Senior** | The first baby I ever delivered. |
| **Junior** | Was it a boy, like this one? |
| **Senior** | Yes. A boy. Born to a mother who was little more than a girl herself. |
| **Junior** | Do you ever wonder what became of them; the babies you delivered? |
| **Senior** | Not usually. But this one, my first, I wonder about him. |
| **Junior** | Perhaps he grew up to ... change the world. |
| **Senior** | Change the world that I brought him into. God knows it needs changing. |
| **Junior** | I don't know why everyone doesn't want to do our job. |
| **Senior** | They can't take the responsibility. |
| **Junior** | Of bringing life? |

**Senior**     Of taking life. From the womb. From the only place on earth where it isn't judged, measured, governed, ruled, restricted. The womb doesn't set standards. It just accepts the child that grows there. Surrounds it, protects it. Even when it leaves, the womb never really lets go of its own. Make the world more like the womb, then they'll all want to be midwives.

**Junior**     And his name, your first baby. Do you remember his name?

**Senior**     Yes. Yes, I remember his name. It was Judas. His name was Judas.


END

# 10. STARLIGHT EXPRESSED

## Characters

**Watcher**
*A casual observer of the stars.*
**Passer-by**
*A Passer by, obviously not known to the other.*

*Watcher stands looking up at the night sky. Passer-by enters and stands near.*

**Watcher**    Stars always look, I don't know ... brighter, at Christmas.

**Passer-by**    Yes. Why is that, do you think?

**Watcher**    I don't know. I suppose it's the only time we really think about them.

**Passer-by**    I like the twinkly red and green ones. Like that one there.

**Watcher**    I think that's an aeroplane.

**Passer-by**    Is it? I wondered why it kept moving.

**Watcher**    Like the Christmas star, you mean.

**Passer-by**    Do I?

**Watcher**    Yes. You know. 'Star of wonder, star of light'. *(Quoting from the carol.)* 'Westward leading still proceeding.'

**Passer-by**    And if we followed the twinkly red and green one; where would that lead us, I wonder?

**Watcher**    Gatwick.

**Passer-by**   Which is it then; this ... what did you call it, 'star of wonder'?

**Watcher**   You can't see it, no. It's err ... not up there. No. Shame really.

**Passer-by**   Never mind. There's plenty of others.

**Watcher**   Yes, but that one ... I mean, that would be proof, wouldn't it?

**Passer-by**   Proof of what?

**Watcher**   The story; The baby in the manger, God in our world. Everything.

**Passer-by**   And you want proof?

**Watcher**   Not for me, no ...

**Passer-by**   But for everyone else, yes. It is a difficult age. Then why the star? Why not the original manger, a piece of frankincense, a feather from an angel's wing?

**Watcher**   I don't mean a relic, I mean ...

**Passer-by**   *(Looking silently up at the sky.)* Do you know how long it takes their light to reach us? Millions of years. We can see it, but it's just a relic from a long time ago. Doesn't prove they're real now.

**Watcher**   Yes, but the light still shines.

**Passer-by**   Not up there. Those stars are dead, finished.

**Watcher**   Shines down here though.

41

**Passer-by**   Exactly. So stop trying to prove the past, and start enlightening the present. *(Returns to looking silently up at the sky for a moment ...)* I still like the twinkly red and green ones best. Not bad, considering.

**Watcher**   Considering what?

**Passer-by**   Well. Considering they're the only ones I didn't make.

*Passer-by has made his exit before Watcher realises he has gone.*

END

# 11. THE EXILE

## Characters

**The Exile**
*An anonymous city dweller on the Underground.*
**Shoppers & Commuters**
*Any number of other passengers.*
**Tannoy** *(Optional)*
*An offstage announcement to emphasise the circular nature of Exile's journey.*

*Exile enters. He has attempted to dress smartly, but by the style and condition of his clothes, and by his general appearance, circumstances are clearly against him. He carries no bags or luggage.*

**Tannoy**    This station is Aldgate. This station is Aldgate. Please mind the gap. Please mind the gap.

*A large number of other people enter. They are well dressed and in a hurry. Some are clearly business people on their way to, or from, work. Others have been Christmas shopping. They pack tightly together around the **Exile**, as if squashed into an overcrowded underground train. They do not interact with each other or with the **Exile**.*

**Exile**    *(Addresses the audience.)* I'm going home for Christmas. I go home every Christmas. Of course, I haven't told them; the family. I never do. I like to surprise them. They appreciate that; the surprise. You can see it on their faces. My mum, dad. Sarah and Jayne. Especially Jayne. Sarah'll have a family of her own by now, of course, but she'll still like to come home.

For Christmas.

It's always like this. *(Indicating the press around him.)* They keep promising us new trains, but ...

It'll be turkey of course. Well, it wouldn't be Christmas, would it? Not without turkey. And those little sausages wrapped in bacon. 'Pigs in blankets' Jayne calls them.

Funny.

Doesn't go all the way; this train. You have to change. To the over-ground. You have to get off.

I've got presents. I wouldn't go without presents. Something pretty for mum, cigars for dad. He likes a cigar after his dinner. And a drink. A scarf for Sarah, and gloves for Jayne. I think. Small. Red. Or blue ... Blue, yeah.

They call it the Circle Line. It's the yellow one. It doesn't actually go anywhere. You can stay on it all day. It just keeps going round.

Crackers.

I might get some crackers. Good ones; with proper things inside. And jokes, and hats that don't tear. And we'll watch the Queen ... if it's still on. And eat chocolate. And we won't fight. We won't. Not once.

I don't have to go home, of course. I could go anywhere. I got lots of friends. In the city. They all ask me; 'what you doing for Christmas?' 'Going home', I said. 'The family'. Well it's sort of expected, isn't it?

And it'll be just like it used to be.

*The other people hurry away as if leaving the train.* **Exile** *is left standing alone.*

Don't worry about me. I always have a great Christmas. I do. But I always put money in the box. You know, for them. 'Cos some people, they don't have a home for Christmas. Can't imagine that. No ... Can't imagine that.

**Tannoy**     This station is Aldgate. This station is Aldgate. Please mind the gap. Please mind the gap.

*The other people return in same hurry and recreate the overcrowded underground train, packing in tightly around the* **Exile**. *As far as possible, the scene should be exactly the same as it was at the beginning of the sketch.*

**Exile**     I'm going home for Christmas.

END

# 12. WHAT TO DO WITH THE LEFTOVERS

Characters
***Sales***
*Sales assistant at ' Christmases Direct'*
***Shopper***
*Shopping for a new Christmas*
***Partner***
*Shopper's male partner*

***Shopper*** *and her* ***Partner*** *enter 'Christmases Direct', a designer Christmas store for the well off.* ***Sales*** *greets them. He has his store catalogue to hand.*

**Sales**      Morning Sir, Madam.

**Shopper**   Good morning.

**Sales**      Is there anything I can show you?

**Partner**   Yes, we're rather looking to buy a Christmas.

**Sales**      Then you've come to the right place. Was there any particular ... style of Christmas you had in mind?

**Shopper**   Well ... we don't really know, do we?

**Partner**   Something a bit different ...

**Shopper**   Yes. Something with a sort of theme to it.

**Sales**      You want a Christmas makeover. They're very popular these days, very popular. Let's just see what we've got here shall we ...?

*Sales flips through his catalogue and shows the chosen page to his customers.*

**Sales**      Ah ... how about this?

**Partner**    A Victorian Christmas?

**Sales**      Yes. Very reliable and guaranteed to impress. German fir tree, carols, holly wreaths, figgy pudding, mulled wine ... *(flips over the page.)*

**Shopper**    Well that sounds lovely.

**Sales**      ... child labour, urban squalor and public hangings.

**Partner**    Oh dear.

**Sales**      Or there's a Medieval Christmas, that's just coming in. That's erm ... partridge, quail, travelling minstrels ... *(flips the page again.)* bubonic plague, mass starvation and bloody religious war.

**Shopper**    Haven't you got something a bit more ... civilised.

**Sales**      *(Searching the catalogue.)* Tricky. Let's see ... we've got twentieth century revolutionary Russian; sort of a ... blood on snow motif. Seventeenth century Puritan English; that's repression and political infighting ... and then there's twenty-first century Australian beach.

**Partner**    That one, the beach one. What about that?

**Sales**      Well that's ... A barbecue lunch on the barrier reef, followed by scuba diving, and volleyball on the sun-kissed coral sands! *(Triumphant.)*

**Partner**   *(Used to this now.)* And?

**Sales**   Salmonella and skin cancer.

**Shopper**   Look, have you got anything that's just a straightforward Christmas, with no wars, no diseases, no urban squalor and no ... unpleasant side effects.

**Sales**   Errm ... no.

**Shopper**   This is hopeless.

**Partner**   Just tell us what most of your customers do, and we'll have one of those.

**Sales**   DIY.

**Partner**   DIY Christmas?

**Sales**   Do it yourself. Yes.

**Shopper**   Can you do that?

**Sales**   Oh, yes. It's quite simple, really. All you do is pick the bits you like from all the others; Medieval banquet, Victorian tree, carols ... on the beach. Just put them all together.

**Partner**   Well that sounds perfect.

**Shopper**   Yes.

**Partner**   We'll take one of those, please.

**Sales**      Certainly. *(He produces a large box with items of Christmas paraphernalia sticking out through the top.)* There you are. And a Merry Christmas to you both.

**Partner**    Thank you.

**Shopper**    Before we go ... what happens to the rest?

**Sales**      Rest?

**Shopper**    The leftovers. The bits we ... don't want.

**Sales**      Oh, you mean the disease, war ... child labour and so on.

**Shopper**    Yes.

**Sales**      We're very generous. We donate them.

**Partner**    Donate them?

**Sales**      Well, some people can't afford a designer Christmas of their own.

**Shopper**    Oh, come on. Really?

**Sales**      Yes, really. Mostly in the third world, of course, so you don't need to worry.

**Partner**    Grateful for anything we can give them, I suppose. Even our leftovers.

**Sales**      Some of them are so grateful, they make the things *you* don't want last all year.

**Shopper**   Imagine that. It must be like Christmas every day.

**Partner**   Some people don't know they're born.

**Shopper**   Well I hope they know who they have to thank for all they get.

**Sales**   I'm sure they do, Madam. I'm sure they do.

## END

# 13. PATERNITY TEST

Characters
***Father***
*A putative father*
***Son***
*His putative son*
***Technician***
*A white-coated scientist*

***Father*** *and* ***Son*** *are waiting for the result of a paternity test.*

**Father**   Why do we have to do this.

**Son**   Because they want us to. They need to be certain.

**Father**   It won't be certain. It will only be a probability.

**Son**   If it's positive.

**Father**   If. You think it might not be?

**Son**   It doesn't matter what I think anymore.

**Father**   And your mother?

**Son**   She is my mother. That's the one thing they are certain about.

**Father**   And what if it's negative? What if this ... 'paternity test' is negative?

**Son**   Then it's over.

**Father**    Is it? Is that all there is to fatherhood; DNA? The passing of genes from one generation to the next?

**Son**    You know there's more to it than that.

**Father**    Yes. But this is for them, isn't it? There's a lot riding on it for them. They've backed you this far, after all. Staked their souls on it, as it were.

**Son**    They just want proof, that's all.

**Father**    I never called anyone son, or daughter, except as a father.

**Son**    And I never called you father except as a son.

**Father**    No. Not 'father'. You never called me that. 'Abba', that's what you called me. 'Abba'. 'Daddy'. No one ever called me that. Except you. Not Abraham, not Moses, not Mohammed. But you, you called me 'daddy'.

*Technician enters. She carries a sealed, plain white envelope; clearly the results of the paternity test. She hands the envelope to Son, who takes it. She gives Father and Son a polite but noncommittal smile, and leaves.*

Go on then. Show it to them. It might tell them if I'm your father. But it won't tell them why you're my son.

**Son**    Perhaps it's better that they don't know.

**Father**    No. It's important that they do. I've never kept anything from them.

**Son**    But if it's positive …

**Father**    Then you will have shown them what it is to be my son.

**Son**    And if it's negative?

**Father**    Then you will have shown them what it is to be my son.

**Son**    And then?

**Father**    Their souls will still be safe, if that's what you mean.

**Son**    Then it doesn't matter?

**Father**    What matters is whether they fully accept me as their father, as completely as you did.

**Son**    Will they do that?

**Father**    I never intended you to be an only child.

## END

# 14. POLICY REVIEW

Characters
### *Welfare*
*Welfare officer for staff facing a new hardship.*
### *Resources*
*Director of Policy for Human Resources (HR).*

**Resources** *has just informed* **Welfare** *of his decision and is closing the meeting.*

**Welfare**    I'm not asking you to do anything. Just to see it from their point of view.

**Resources**    And then what?

**Welfare**    Well ... try and include them. Heaven knows they've suffered enough.

**Resources**    Staff welfare is your business. Human Resources department has more important things to worry about.

**Welfare**    They're not resources, they're people. They have families, children.

**Resources**    Do you know what this project is worth? Have you any idea what it will mean to this company, this town. This ... country?

**Welfare**    It's Christmas. Can't you at least wait until the new year? What's a few more weeks for something of this size?

**Resources**    You really have no idea, do you? We've got to protect ourselves. If we hold back now, it'll look like weakness.

There'll be a crisis of confidence, the share holders will panic, the banks will pull out. We could lose it all.

**Welfare**    They're going to lose it all anyway.

**Resources**  So why make things worse?

**Welfare**    Why not make things better?

**Resources**  I am making things better.

**Welfare**    They're losing their jobs, their livelihoods.

**Resources**  These are details. I'm concerned with policy, not details.

**Welfare**    Look, they don't deserve this.

**Resources**  And you want me to reward the undeserving? What kind of Human Resources policy is that?

**Welfare**    A Christmas one; a compassionate one.

*There is a pause in the argument **Resources** looks hard at **Welfare**, then produces a cheque book and writes out a cheque.*

**Resources**  Look. I'm not unsympathetic. Here's a cheque made out to the hardship fund. Fill in the amount yourself. *(Hands over the cheque.)*

**Welfare**    *(Reading the cheque.)* This isn't a corporate cheque.

**Resources**  Of course it's not. It's a personal cheque. On my account.

**Welfare**    It's alright for you to show compassion but not the company.

**Resources**   We don't have a policy on compassion.

**Welfare**   Then perhaps we should.

**Resources**   Compassion isn't a corporate thing.

**Welfare**   Even at Christmas?

**Resources**   Especially at Christmas. It's all personal. Kings, shepherds, wise men. All personal. Show me one act of corporate policy in the whole story. You can't. There isn't one.

**Welfare**   Not even the slaughter of the innocents?

**Resources**   That was Herod …

**Welfare**   It was the establishment protecting itself. Isn't that an act of corporate policy?

**Resources**   Hey, look. If you're trying to say …

**Welfare**   … that nothing's changed.

**Resources**   He slaughtered babies, for heaven's sake. We're just letting go of a few dozen office staff.

**Welfare**   The motive's the same; power, profit, prestige …

**Resources**   You've really lost it this time.

**Welfare**   No. Look. Supposing you don't let them go. Supposing you face this thing *with* them instead of without them.

**Resources**   It's not policy.

**Welfare**     Then change the policy.

**Resources**   What? You can't just change policy. That would mean changing everything. It'd be like … changing the whole world.

**Welfare**     Perhaps that's why Christmas needs to be all personal. At least to start with.

*Welfare takes the cheque from **Resources** and leaves him standing alone.*

END

# 15. THEOLOGY STORY

## Characters
### Principal
*of a theological college, seminary or other school for ministers.*
### Chancellor
*of the same.*

*The **Principal** and **Chancellor** have just finished interviewing a candidate for their college. They address the audience as though they were that candidate.*

**Principal**  Don't think we're unsympathetic.

**Chancellor**  We'd love to have you. Really, we would.

**Principal**  It's just that, well, we can't let just anyone in, can we?

**Chancellor**  If we did that we'd have to have everyone. And that would never do.

**Principal**  And once you're in, it could be very difficult to get you out.

**Chancellor**  But we do like your ideas.

**Principal**  At least, we think we do.

**Chancellor**  But we're not *quite* sure.

**Principal**  In fact, we're not *quite* sure … about you.

**Chancellor**  You haven't really told us very much about yourself.

**Principal**  All we know for certain is that you were born.

**Chancellor**  Everything else ...

**Principal**  ... Date, time, place ... parentage ...

**Chancellor**  ... Reads like some sort of story.

**Principal**  Which is really our problem.

**Chancellor**  You see, in our line, people expect something ... solid.

**Principal**  Rules, doctrines, instruction. That sort of thing.

**Chancellor**  And all you give them ... is stories.

**Principal**  Stories.

**Chancellor**  Some of which, you don't even bother to explain properly.

**Principal**  And how do we know what they mean if you don't explain them properly?

**Chancellor**  Because if you don't explain them, people ... some people ... might make up their minds for themselves.

**Principal**  And we're sure you don't want that, do you?

**Chancellor**  Do you?

**Principal**  So we're sorry. But we're going to have to turn you down.

**Chancellor**  Still, never mind. Theological college isn't for everyone, is it?

**Principal**  Preaching the Good News; it's something you're either *born* to, or you're not, Mr … what did you say your name was?

## END

# Nimbus Press Titles

available from Nimbus Press, 18 Guilford Road, Leicester LE2 2RB
Tel: 0116 270 6318    www.nimbuspress.co.uk

## Various authors

*PLATFORM SOULS – Gospel Sketches for the New Millennium*
*SKETCHES FOR SEEKER SERVICES: 1*
*SKETCHES FOR SEEKER SERVICES: 2*
*CELEBRATING LIGHT – Sketches for Churches on the theme of 'light'*

## Edward Bennett

*LETS GO TO BETHLEHEM*
*FULL HOUSE IN BETHLEHEM*
*GOOD NEWS IN BETHLEHEM*
*THE ROSE HAS THORNS  – a play for Easter*

## Stephen Deal

*MAKING WAVES*
*KINGDOM AIRWAYS*
*SHORT CHANGE*

## Les Ellison

*FIRST EASTER – Nine Holy Week dramas*
*AWAY FROM THE MANGER - Christmas sketches*

## Rosi MorganBarry

*ANGEL'S COUNSEL – a true Christmas 'Fairytale'*

## Ronald Rich

*EVEN MORE SURPRISE SKETCHES*
*TIME TO SPEAK   – a play about Pilate and Peter 30 years on*

## Clifford Sharp/Jonathan Curnow

*THE GOLDEN AGE – an environmental play*
*THE PRICE OF OLIVES – a play about Jesus' family life*
*MY KIND OF GOD – two short plays*
*IS THIS YOUR LIFE? & PEARL OF GREAT PRICE*
*THE GOOD CHURCH GUIDE – who's the best?*
*LOOKING FOR A KING – two short Christmas Plays*

## Non - Drama

*NOT IN FRONT OF THE CHILDREN - how to present Christmas honestly.*
*IT HAPPENED TO A CHRISTIAN – true funny and sad stories*